JAZZ MASTERS

Charlie Parker

JAZZ MASTERS

Charlie Parker

by Stuart Isacoff

Consolidated Music Publishers

New York • London • Tokyo • Sydney • Cologne

Cover design by Carol Zimmerman
Cover photo by David Gahr

Order No. AM 27004
US International Standard Book Number: 0.8256.4081.4

Exclusive Distributors:
Music Sales Corporation
257 Park Avenue South, New York, NY 10010 USA
Music Sales Limited
8/9 Frith Street, London W1V 5TZ England
Music Sales Pty. Limited
120 Rothschild Street, Rosebery, Sydney, NSW 2018, Australia

Printed in the United States of America by
Vicks Lithograph and Printing Corporation

Contents

Charlie Parker (1920-1955)

The story of jazz consists of more than just the pitches and rhythms of its punching drums and staggering melodies. It arose from the lives of men and women who invested this music with a fierce energy and a relentless striving for the seemingly unreachable. One such man was Charlie Parker—"Bird"— and few musicians have left as deep and as lasting an effect on the technique and style of contemporary music.

As a boy, Parker listened to Lester Young in the Kansas City clubs where Coleman Hawkins, Ben Webster and other giants met for "cutting sessions"— contests to determine the best improviser. It was during such a session that Parker, tenor saxophone in hand, first stepped forward to publicly negotiate the turns and hurdles of a set of "chord changes"; the tune was "Body and Soul" and the response was laughter. It was not to be the last time he would find himself in such painful circumstances. At another session drummer Jo Jones stopped playing just long enough to hurl a cymbal at Bird, who had become lost on a chorus of "I Got Rhythm."

Such events only strengthened Parker's resolve to become the best. Whether he was washing dishes for $9 a week at the Chicken Shack (where the great Art Tatum played nightly) or playing saxophone at a 10¢-a-dance joint on Broadway, his goal remained firm: to release the music that lay locked somewhere in his heart and mind, a music never before heard in the world of jazz.

Bird's competence and reputation as an alto saxophonist grew year by year. His technical facility and experimental daring produced an approach which made use of chromatic movement in a new and surprising way. Earlier jazz artists had played quick flurries of notes, but these were generally arpeggios or linear scale-like groupings; Parker created a style based on playing many notes per chord in a wholly melodic fashion. In order to craft these endlessly weaving lines he had to reach to the highest partials of each chord, producing momentary dissonances which moved by with lightning speed; the resulting music was at once strange and delightful. In addition, the endings of many of his phrases suggested a modal rather than tonal feeling, so that even in its resting spots the melodic contour held surprises for the listener. Parker's skill in molding these melodies increased to the point that he became known for composing magnificent tunes on the spot, pausing only seconds at a recording session to jot them down for the other musicians.

But the pain of his life outweighed the beauty of his creations. Bird began to drink, treating his peptic ulcers with a combination of milk and scotch; then he turned to heroin as a way to wipe out the world. (At one point he signed away half his record royalties for a small amount of heroin. The dealer unsuccessfully attempted to collect the money by mail from his prison cell.)

He did maintain his sense of humor, though, and it sometimes took an existential turn, as when he ate the petals of the rose a fan presented to him, and then placed the bud in his lapel. Such an action was as incomprehensible to his audience as his strange harmonies were to older muscians. On another occasion, upon meeting philosopher Jean-Paul Sartre, Bird said, "I'm very glad to have met you. I like your playing very much."

Bird's brilliance, coupled with a bitterness toward life, spawned several notorious encounters with club owners and fellow musicians. Toward the end of his life, he had a fight on stage with pianist Bud Powell which reached such embarrassing proportions that bassist Charles Mingus walked to the microphone and asked the audience to disassociate him from the group. Backstage, Bird was filled with sadness. "Mingus," he said, "I'm goin' someplace, pretty soon, where I'm not gonna bother anybody."

A Note on the Transcriptions

In this edition, for C instruments, the solos have been transcribed at concert pitch, to read as they originally sounded. These transcriptions may be played on any nontransposing instrument, such as piano, guitar, flute, violin, trombone, etc. A separate edition (Music for Millions Series 90/040090) is available which contains the same material transposed for E♭ alto saxophone.

The first six solos in this book, "Oop Bop Sh-Bam," "Good Dues Blues," "One Bass Hit," "Ray's Idea," "That's Earl, Brother," and "Things To Come," are taken from a publication entitled *Be-Bop Instrumental Choruses for Alto Sax* published by J.J. Robbins & Sons in 1949. These "6 original choruses on outstanding be-bop themes" were actually arranged by Charlie Parker and transcribed by Walter "Gil" Fuller.

Oop Bop Sh-Bam

By "Dizzy" Gillespie, Walter Fuller and Jay Roberts

Good Dues Blues

By "Dizzy" Gillespie, Ray Brown and Walter Fuller

One Bass Hit

By "Dizzy" Gillespie, Ray Brown and Walter Fuller

Ray's Idea

By Ray Brown and Walter Fuller

That's Earl, Brother

By "Dizzy" Gillespie, Ray Brown and Walter Fuller

Things To Come

By "Dizzy" Gillespie and Walter Fuller

Hot House

By Tadd Dameron

I'll Remember April

By Don Raye, Gene De Paul and Pat Johnston

52nd Street Theme

By Thelonious Monk

Out Of Nowhere

By Edward Heyman and Johnny Green

Bird Of Paradise

By Charlie Parker

DUKE JORDAN

3. BIRD

A Night In Tunisia

By "Dizzy" Gillespie and Frank Paparelli

Bongo Bop

By Charlie Parker

Groovin' High

By "Dizzy" Gillespie

Discography

Jazz At Massey Hall
Fantasy LFR-8849

Hot House

A Night In Tunisia

Charlie Parker With Strings
Verve MV-2562

I'll Remember April

Charlie Parker, Vol. 3: Groovin' High
SAGA Records ERO-8007

52nd Street Theme

Groovin' High

Charlie Parker On Dial, Vol. 5
Odeon EOR-9032

Out Of Nowhere

Charlie Parker On Dial, Vol. 4
Odeon EOR-9031

Bird of Paradise

Bongo Bop